AF478460

Flares And Fathoms

POEMS BY MARGOT FARRINGTON

*For Sharon —
another voice I heard
and thought should
be heeded —
with my thanks,
Margot Farrington
4/6/06*

Bright Hill Press
Treadwell, New York
2005

Flares and Fathoms

Poems by Margot Farrington

Selected by Bright Hill Press

Bright Hill Press
Poetry Book Series, No. 2

Book Design: Bertha Rogers
Cover Art: Tony Martin, "Departure of Whim"
Editor in Chief: Bertha Rogers
Editorial Staff: Ernest M. Fishman
Copyright © 2005 by Margot Farrington
First Edition

Library of Congress Cataloging-in-Publication Data

Farrington, Margot.
  Flares and fathoms : poems / by Margot Farrington.
     p. cm. -- (Bright Hill Press poetry series ; no. 2)
  ISBN 1-892471-30-2 (alk. paper).
  I. Title. II. Series.

  PS3606.A738F57 2005
  811'.6--dc22

                                              2005012004

Flares and Fathoms is published by Bright Hill Press
Bright Hill Press, Inc., a not-for-profit, 501©)(3) literary and educational organization, was founded in 1992. The organization is registered with the New York State Department of State, Office of Charities Registration. Publication of *Flares and Fathoms* is made possible, in part, with public funds from the Literature Program of the New York State Council on the Arts, a State Agency.

Editorial Address
Bright Hill Press, Inc.
94 Church Street, POB 193
Treadwell, NY 13846-0193
Voice / Fax: 607-829-5055
Web Site: www.brighthillpress.org
E-mail: wordthur@stny.rr.com

All rights reserved. Except for brief quotation in critical articles or reviews, this book, or parts thereof, must not be reproduced in any form or by any means, electronic or mechanical, including photocopy, recording, or any information storage and retrieval system, without permission in writing from the publisher. Requests for permission to make copies of any part of the work should be mailed to Bright Hill Press, 94 Church Street, POB 193, Treadwell, NY 13846-0193.

ACKNOWLEDGMENTS

Grateful acknowledgment is made to the following journals, magazines, and anthologies for poems that originally appeared in them:

Heliotrope: "Denial"
Pembroke Magazine: "Evening"
Poetry Wales (UK): "The Book Of Fireworks," "Work," "For Sale," "Voodoo"
Outerbridge: "The Snakes"
The Brooklyn Rail: "Blizzard: Brooklyn View"
Best Poems of Outerbridge 1991-2001: "The Snakes"
The Word Thursdays Anthology Of Poetry And Fiction (Bright Hill Press): "Lightning"

"People In The Wind" was produced as a limited-edition broadside in 2002 by Bright Hill Press for the exhibition "Words For 9/11" at the Word and Image Gallery, Bright Hill Center, Treadwell, New York. The poem also appeared on the Academy of American Poets web site, www.poets.org, under *New Spring Books*, for National Poetry Month 2005.

For Tony

CONTENTS

I

DARK / LIGHT

BED

Barque that bears the past, afloat
on the spindrift of dreams,
you shipwreck for the move
into side rails, seven slats, into
headboard, footboard, box spring,
a mattress that's seen action.

"My grandmother's." Nothing more
need be said, I know. Rodrigo and Segundo
nod. Matched jaguars, they heft my
history, pad down two flights
and, in the truck,
pack those mahogany bones as though
they were their own.

Away. Away to another house,
exchanging brick for clapboard. Trading sparrow for thrush,
traffic's rush for a stream.

And it's I—on this end—who
carries what I can upstairs,
still in my prime, last of a line of
women willful and defined by some
green music that in youth was hope
and later, harnessed fevers
that in age may hold both spark and smolder
until, like them, I'm over and this bed begins anew,
red-gold in a sun-struck room,
sturdy as the man who made it.
He whistled, perhaps. Blackbird notes.
The work went well; he was in love.

A Field Of Speedwell

Akin in power
to lightning's illusory sleight-of-hand,
the first glimpse alters where
you stand, who you thought you were.

Balm and scorch commingled. Marriage
of fountain with flame, their
aftermath of violet tightening in your throat. You
cannot breathe; you breathe for the
first time in years.

Strange yet apt the name for
that flower of seven fathoms. Yours
the rising to the surface
in that narcotic hue

And you mount the
horse of no hoof prints and you ride,
ageless and blithe.

Falling Asleep

      You never would   it seemed
but shuddered
and quivered
one tremor after another took you
everyone had your ear
and what they whispered
was not good
what they whispered
charged electric
fields all over your skin
ran the cinema across your face

it was there the worst scenes raged
families died and lovers lost
the sea in its fury
could never be calmed   could never

suddenly   on the intake
your breath gathered all corners
north   *no not there*
south east   *help me*   west
held oh   held   then flattened
to silence lasting so long   your

fingers touched a marble angel's lips
(powdered she was   powdered with golden lichen)
you tried for a word
but no word would come

at last you breathed again
   they resumed whispering
and you who craved a moment's respite

sought to hear beyond the dense
graffiti of their utterance

what you were doing there   between
one second's lash and
the next   what were you doing   what were you
and without answer
slept.

DOWNPOUR

No matter. Here it comes.
Don't run inside—it's too late.
The darkest cloud's announced a number,
the band's about to begin.
    Stay put. Hold out
your glass for chardonnay.
    Note the

lilacs, who will later (and altogether)
take slow bows. See their
leaves: little cymbals struck, just so.
    The past too, is percussive,
and rarely lets up.

See how they strike then
    jump, these drops. Each by each is
mimed. Lift your face,
(streaked before sky
turned and foretold) toward
the roofs. There rivulets wild and
gutter-tamed prove more than match
for yours. Mark how
thunder utters one phrase
though you're keyed for more.

Get up, commands your heart,
forswear this world gone indigo.
Love, my love, the rain keeps saying.
Drink up, endure.

LIGHTNING

When wind comes, it comes like wolves
with a strategy, turning the trees expertly and
circling with intent. Running relays with an easy
power. This is the hunt that parts the air
for the sequence of lightning, wind everywhere,
pulling resistance down wherever it finds some.

Then lightning, bodiless but for a huge
pair of hands, bodiless and yet with a fine
acrobat's presence, grips a bar no one can see
and vaults across the landscape, bleaching the hills,
bringing the barns forward a furtive step.

We're driving home in separate cars, though as
lightning vaults again, I feel these hills
might be the hills of Mars or of memory,
childhood hills or some valley Death secretly
folded us into, so that we travel
without knowing we've left our lives behind.

I follow you, thinking of Violet Kennedy, who was
struck by lightning and survived; of how pale
she was, as if the bolt had stolen all her natural color,
but charged—before leaving her body—
her blue eyes bluer as a gift. And how if lightning
could be attracted on the basis of names, surely
a strong choice would be Violet: a flower so firmly
of the ground, its color the color of lightning's heart.

In mind's eye, I see our room, lit in detail
from two windows. Lightning illuminates furrows
in the cloth of the bedspread, the dark chair
whose startled legs leap to support the seat at each flash.

~

The marble top of the bedside table levitates, the
shade of the small lamp trembles like a bell.

And who will I find at home when I pull
into the driveway, where the parked red car,
the house, the maples, stutter in and out of existence?
You'll already be in our room, a dear familiar stranger.
Your face as the flash finds you and
imprints you in my brain, will hold the
brevity of our lives brightly before me,
moving me towards you in terror and love
to touch you before the light goes.

THE BOOK OF FIREWORKS

I

The First

What do you say when Golden Lonely
goes up, destined for his own heavens?

Delayed, but you heard in your head
red strike rough, and the match exclaim.

Hurry, tonight is impetuous.
Answer these three questions.

How high is too far? What is suspense if not
darkness? Where exactly does the arc

falter, exhale with cadenced flurries
those ordered, forgetful stars and

sorry, time's up for the answers and for this
impostor among comets, conceived in a tube,

waking to life as blown thistle.

II

Different Views

The Red One said death by pleasure.
The Blue One said death of pain.
The Green said seizure. And Gold?
Everyone's crazy.
    The Gold & Silver: No one's to blame.

Next volley, Red said spend it.
The Blue, better luck.
I'll stand this round. (Green, of course).
Gold said, I'm swinging—duck!
Silver faked, brought out a bloom
    of interior blue.
Translation proved difficult, was it:
Let this be a lesson to you?

Sssssssst! Red. Basic.
. . . my one regret, finished Blue.
Unintelligible from Green.
Silver's remark rang as untrue.
A better effort. Red again.
Pfffffttt. Intervening dud.
A handful of stars dithering whitely
before the Great Unseen.

III

The Preparations

They studied stones chucked into water,
the blowhole of the whale. They noted the eye
narrowed in cunning, the nipple's contraction
under passion. And the mole's eruption into daylight:
a word heaved out of earth.

They slammed doors, observed bells in wind
not strong enough to ring them. They ruptured pillows
to study the drift of down. For the stopwatch
ground beneath a boot heel, they listened as one.
All walked into the lake with lit cigars in hand.

They traced the lines of wood engravings, tried
hypnosis with a potter's wheel. They scattered sequins
in a game they called Find The Constellations—this while
drinking wine, while trading hats. From a balcony, they
dropped teacups to the floor below.
Lastly, they listened to opera, to their children sobbing.

Then they were ready; they filed into the
blankness of the field. With each fuse was packed a day.
The calendar lay stacked. The night sky made them
shiver, and all the faces they couldn't see: lovers
parked in cars halfway up the hill.
A year. Another year.
A kiss before you go, they thought.

People In The Wind

Inside the wood stove the smith steadies,
proclaims his alliance with flame as
heat quickens his hammer. And the singer, at first
inaudible, fashions her rising song from seasons
stored within logs of seasoned cherry, beech.

I have delighted in their concert
winter days and nights, rapt before
doors framed in brass, their
glass etched with twin wreaths. Circles
that focused wonders I am about to mention:
livid saints and salamanders,
paraphernalia of magicians
performing—with blue fluidity—
their act without their masters.
   And always before curtain, the casket
split asunder, the thief's hand passing over
unattainable gems.

But now there are people in the wind;
the chimney sucks them down. I hear the
singer inhale a choir: voice of thousands.
A purity of anguish to leave the listener
breathless. The notes, the notes are inferno;
the smith beats out a knell.
Those ashes I spill tomorrow
upon freshly fallen snow
have already blown for days across the city.

Blizzard: Brooklyn View

A man shovels in a parking lot
for a car supposedly there
but the car so loves its burial
he gives up and goes,
engulfed in swan's down, Florentine swirls,
the ticker tape of heaven.

To sparse trees comes a minimal spring,
precise and oriental: three blooms here,
four there, birds brown and blood-red.
Bricks take on the texture of
their mortar; shingles show as if newly cut.
Traffic? What is traffic?
People? There are no people.
The ornate wind, thousand-flaked, leaps from
building to building. Softly the
neighborhood alters to a mock Siberian scene,
swathed in ermine,
capped with repeated conical hats.

Good people, kept home today
from your various jobs, look out your windows,
grasp what might be a
metaphor for love:
simplicity in a deepening world.

II

A PORTHCAWL NOTEBOOK

Dog's Mercury

Up to the knees in dog's mercury,
he said,
though we weren't, we stood instead by fading
bluebells, ferns—and here and there—the twayblade, and
everywhere an aquarium light
filtering through a copse of hazels.

Dog's mercury. What a name.
It triggered ambush behind my eyes. A leaf so molten
movement conjured queen silver of no-silvers.
Underpinned with bronze.

Only in stillness of the interval after,
might the dazzled draw close, discover ovate leaves
showing a delicate tooth. Multitudes clasped to
claret stems where—emerging from leafstalk's kink—
the calyx sports a trio: small, easy to miss.
   Those flowers opt out of any one sire:
born russet, ivory, or cunningly
brindled, and over their lips run little red
stamens of woodland laughter.
They're intense; one of those flowers that's
got a gaze: regard of the fetching dog who waits with
stick held firm. Wholly anticipatory,
ablaze for one act.

Of course, I've made all this up, the plant looks
nothing like that. But, dog's mercury—who could resist
the trip beneath that hat? No sooner uttered,
I went there, witnessed and returned and this
elapsed between space of
mind's lightning and thunder clap.

~

And where I've gone, you tread
through hazels lichened-kissed, their wavery limbs
dappled, angled as you wish. I waver also; a trick
of the light, and here's something you might have
missed: this button fallen from my shirt.
          In the scene (are you still there?)
I step upon it, oblivious,
embed its pearly face firmly in the earth. Your footprints,
following, fit themselves to mine.   The man has
turned back, about to say something else, his
speech sprung from Pen-y-fai, his eyes some
theft from sea or sky and they
          look through me into you.

Wander
          where you will; he is now your guide.

WORK

In the smithy, I've toured her tools,
seen the sculptures of a woman
working iron in what was once the stronghold
of men, and stepping outside
take note of the terrier's
refinement: fresh dig inside
an already cavernous hole
        a crater, really,
worthy adornment for that pocked madam,
the moon

and here's the ambition of pin feathers
pushing out of a gosling's head
body hurrying towards goosedom,
grave regard of its thumbtack eyes
fastened on where we're going

past walls, past
pennywort enhancing its grip in a crack
tiny spires
commanding of me: miss nothing!
as I attempt

on the site of this mill
to imagine
the water wheel—restored—
revolving through the rush
running beneath our feet, keeping my
            balance
upon the plank I find I've
walked out on with others, loving their voices
as the stretching   thread of what they say
            (what are they saying?)
turns gossamer
and snaps.

For Sale

Mortar still tight in the
stones, but the door long bolted. Lift
hands or be stung by the interweave
of nettles in waist-high grass.
    So. How much for history?
What price for faith?

Walk round (this church
hugs itself), regarding windows
too small. Never was sky accommodated,
sunlight made welcome.
Whatever angels were spoken of
have fled and
no pigeons seek this place
though a swarm of bees—fist in chain mail—
clenches high in one corner.
    Focused: the queen's all.

    Year on year advance
until a buyer comes
blind to constraints, who has no fear
of the few dead buried here, nor feels too keenly
God was either shut in or out,
but writes a check (the sum small)
to claim the patience of this place,
these ragged hedgerows,
a morning glory: diminutive gramophone
in the silence between records.

Five Rock Pools

First

Stranded, the tiny
take stage, mostly for no one.
Here dines the
crab, thumbnail sized,
palely transparent.
You call that a shell? I say, but he
waves both forks boldly,
lifts another bit of invisible
feast into his mouth.
Wee gourmand, savoring—with all the
salt of the sea—
something delicious.

Second

Though there's no starfish in view
you sense one pointing out your
mode: backstroke. Or is it butterfly,
never really mastered? Flummoxing stroke
that eluded as you learned to swim.
    And where did you? Keep going. Flutter—not one
      place,
but many. A necklace of pools strung with the
syllables of an instructor's surname:
Jac-o-bee-see. (Never encountered
before or since).
    Did it end with an *i* or an *e*? You've
forgotten. But not those golden
hairs on his arms and legs, his deep chest,
nor that appraising cat, slow,
rim-circling. Morning lessons
in pools chilly and pristine. Shyness
a hand—huge—
covert in its dark glove.
Slipping fingers over your mouth,
a movement towards, away.

Third

This one is Nausica's, daughter of
Alcinous, king of Scheria. Scheria?
     (Corfu to you).
          When will Ulysses—? Never mind,
wait and be patient.
Concentrate.
Close your eyes. Open your mind to this pool.
     Ready? Look again,
past your own face.
Farther.
Deeper. (Some sea nymph
     laughs).
What fool ever told you a little pool
is shallow?

Fourth

Which of us was stillest
before I startled you so?

Hostage until the next tide
you might survive here nicely,
cryptic colors saving the day.

   In my world lives a friend, expert in
sorting silver. I know she would
tell me your eyes are neither
sterling nor plate, but coin.

   In your world you stop
panicking, only the breeze moves.
And your gills, surpassingly subtle
   (did you know I once had gills?).

If this pool was greatly expanded,
if you were of sporting size,
(swim back with me: Moosehead Lake, Maine,
    many years ago),
my wrist would flick
a filament, write on air my signature,
the fly settling like down
on surface ruptured by your
strike.

   Let me confess,
I fish no more; sentiment has me firmly,
and speaking of silver, multiple strands
run rampant in my hair. I've come to love
this earthly existence
too fiercely to pretend I have no

~

fear of what will come for you, for me,
but here's the thing—
we'll be as one; I see our joinery
in the alphabet of amazement,
the letter formed as we're pulled from this
world into—what? Nothing?   Another?
  You and I,
      mouths in tandem: o, my water   O

Fifth

Go on. Take a stone
home. Which will it be? Some say
nothing. Some whisper in
stone sibilance: Choose me.

Out of every possible grey: warm
cool, pitted, smoothed,
smoky, sullen, blue-ticked,
double of ash, of dove pinion,
Confederate, dapple, driftwood
(the list's a sinker, cut from its line)
take from a coastline's crescent this
adventurer. The most
persuasive, the one sporting a white
belly band: circumference of quartz
running wild,
only to close upon itself.

I'm lonely, keep me company.
I'm tired, come sleep in my hand.
Good friends and bitter rivals,
bid the chosen
        good-bye.

FIREWORKS OVER PORTHCAWL

There spread a green wedding band,
ringing a dangerous chasm,
a red-riveted heart
that beat once, then lost shape.
    Next? The sorcerer's chrysanthemums
and alternately, his laughter
between the wit, triple-tiered,
of the village wag. Then? Tiaras we couldn't
wear, and an argument, resurrected,
that burst upon us afresh and we
gasped again from what was
said.
    The kids were tired and
viewed without knowledge which
whirling sperm had engendered them
(those whistled as they fell,
half high note joy, half dirge).

In the dark it was hard to discern
ambition from afterglow,
rage from revelation, with what benevolence or
disdain the ocean received what was left.
    But before they faded, each said to the sky
what the maker intended, while each of us named
them in secret according to our whim:
Fugue To Include The North Star.
The Widow's Exultation. Blues For
Everyone And No One.
Print Of The Lynx In Thaw.

The Lark

I'm sitting by sea's edge where geology
offers a subtle union: limestone
veining sandstone's ruddy pink.
And those notes I listen to
(shivering in the westerlies),
fall like the first I might ever have
heard, profound in this coastal place, this
theater by the sea where tide-carved
creatures of limestone
grimace or gape in awe. Invention is endless here.

A rip tide: that lark's
song ineffably sweet and bold,
loosing my hold on the hour, splaying the
deck of days backwards: faces,
susurrus of numbers laid
down on the long felt surface of life.

I am brought again to that early field
at the end of a dead end street
where the song of another bird pulls
thread through the gloss of privet,
leading me back to an osage orange, bowed,
bearing from countless children
a saddle spot burnished to lucent amber.
No time to climb,
get above this current, though there's a
moment for the tiny graveyard:
five tablets of marble, their lettering
muffled in moss. Whoever is
singing now lets me lay a quick
flower down: one only for the five before the

~

current rushes me on, for music
swells unceasingly
from the singer's throat,
sweeping me back: I grow younger and smaller.
Buckled in a stroller, I
point at sight of a bird,
powerless yet to engrave with English,
to cut into air that word,
though if I uttered words now
they would be those venerable two
shaken out from the folds of a folk tale,
                    question
endlessly asked of the traveler:

            Whither away?   No answer—
only song flashing through
space. I'm an infant babbling a string of
under notes in reverse, vanishing
into the mouths of my
mother and father
caught in a kiss, lost in the welter and
sway of 5 a.m. lovemaking
                    wherein
lies the dark flare. The possibility of
me.

URN AND DOOR

White house with blue urn, blue
door mentally tried
each day or evening of passing by.
Such are fantasy's tickets, the
endless come-on of a curve. Thus
eye will follow arch as finger might trace
eyebrow, dare with tentative touch
the contour of a mouth. For the door's
not rectangular, the urn
empty but for expectation:
coiled wherever
venture and darkness intersect.

Past them, the garden you'll never enter
holds crescent green sharply edged,
calla lilies, a laburnum
shaking down her hair while from the
dolphin's mossed lip drops
sluggish verse for the sea.

Blue—you mean cobalt: the elopement of
midnight to marry noon.
Color at the deep end, playing zither on
your heart. A few obsessive chords,
lyrics compressed to three and three:
Urn equals yearning. Door equals more.

NOTE FROM A FIELD WITHOUT HOUSE

Stone walls giving way, sea just across the
road, these poppies in a broken corner, their
spots bold upon their crepe.
Darling, the only
 paper I have, can you handle the color, not to
 mention how this ink may be
 affecting how I think?

 Was ever a house here?
Wassssevevver, mocks the waking sea,
turning over for the millionth time,
kelp tasseling her hips.

Call it (I write) *the spell cast by absence:*
people tend to linger here. They build a
dream house, garden away their days.
 Fools, I scrawl from the black
Rorschach I can't help dipping in.
 The palms nod. No one passes. My
mind is in leopard's leap,
that is to say, in the tensile
future: wind-rush, no contact yet.

—y love, my pen blorts out, as felt as
rain's first drops. Less pressure, I council
myself, but the petal
                         falls, I move to another.
 My love, this field's value
surpasses all assessment. Only the gold of the
gorse might buy it. If only—my nib rebels—
if o—my nib leaks out—*if left*
alone, (this comma spreads, swallows a
following phrase) *such glory* (third blort)
no one can match (final). *I hope you can*
read this, as I'm out of poppies. Others will
open later, but I'll post this now.

The Cinnabar Moth

A scuff of sand from your boot toe
downs and buries it. I stoop, rise with
    contents for an hourglass,
grains slipping over my palm, sifting
back to the dune like the
salt of centuries. Leaving the moth
becalmed, fabulous in my hand.

What message to take and to
whom, from that heraldic
black and orange? What response to an
answer impudent, wise,
  ruthless or tender, and what the
manner of my punishment or reward?
   Halt! command four portals. Grains go on racing through
my fingers. *One!* hears the moth and
splays a millimeter more. And my eyes—my eyes those
captives of the undescried
              keep crying *Moment!*

  O, I was rich and famous
  O, I was desperate poor
  I bedded on silk and velvet
  I slept on earthen floor
  I never thought to fall from grace
  Nor that death might claim me early
  To see contempt in a lover's face
  But the world treads hard and surly . . . .

How may I face the unforeseen? Wind whips
hair into my eyes, blinded I hear still
the song within its guise as these wings
vivid on the crossroads of my hand
  hesitate.   Leave me riven when they lift,
              flutter away.

Tribute

Collected Works. A big book, probably your last. The
place packed. (Did you bewilder some? Still, they've
turned out). Your son beside you. Your recent
strokes folded keenly within. You wait, the neutral master.
How does this begin?

Not strong enough to read yourself, others will read
chosen selections. Your name's put
forth, rises into the chapel's nave. (You preached, too,
but never here, nor for this denomination).

Difficult to concentrate while focus of attention. Applause
(for what? the introduction?) dies, here comes the
first of your verses, alien and a-scuffle, (he's
scotching the humor, can't get the lines to live, nor
get out of his own way), but there's a bit of feeble laughter
    and

by and by he finishes, sits to the rising of the next, and
    she fares slightly
better. Then comes the third—from him no poems,
only a litany: all you've done, how long he's
known you, Venerable One, how well, how well, how well
    you
wish him gone, though he's a friend, he does not
    speak for you now

will they not cry, sing out your densities hard-
    chiseled, won to clarity?

~

Or is it you, deaf by stress of this hyper-listening,
fox poised between footfalls wherein breathes the
hidden hare? But here's the fourth, and broken open
   by a phrase
that still surprises, you shut your eyes, reinvent it,

mouth it word for word. She comprehends somewhat,
   gives them what she can,
though each poem ducks through the door
of her own importance. She sparks them here and there,
you brave a look around; they're warming to it,
though her fire's of kindling
instead of logs.
                Ah wait, now, wait, this last is a
fellow who knows, who like a blade cuts from the air-page
your poems, newly freed. Christ, the grain of your
desk, your hand, coffee sludge in mug, rain
blearing glass, your wife's knock—dinner would be cold.
Coming! Sharp the labor for what he helps deliver

meanings shapely as those lilies flaring on
the altar: trumpets and silence, green within white,
wildness within the carefully bred, and something of
pulpit wood tree-dreaming, of stone mastered
   or left alone.
All anyone ever wants: to be understood,
   heard as intended.
All you could ask of this ventriloquism, eerie but
satisfying, that voice honing in,
clear enough. Close.

Crosscuts: St. Teilo
(two riding mowers in attendance)

   No gardeners need apply.
For this insolence of grass you
need drivers, gasoline.
We'll ride those masses down
with regulated passes.

•

Upon faces of celtic stones
lichen imitates old friends:
snowflake   flower
cloud concealing its inner cloud.

•

Our scythe's a pair of strimmers.
Hand clippers? Strictly history.
Yew and yew and yew:
get back against the wall.

•

Who last cat-footed to the clerestory,
past saints in leaded glass? This sunlight
stains you, seeker, into wearing motley:
a slippage harking back as far as
14th century. Whose gaze might you dare
meet? And what do you read there:
forgiveness or melancholy?

•

Once this churchyard relied upon
teeth of sheep. Later, some gardener.
Think how long it took him, while with
us it takes just an hour.

   Let me remind you, began the quatrefoil
   carved above church door. Surely a splendid
      speech,
   lost to the doubled roar of mowers.

THE JACKDAW

Dice swirled in sky's cup, this
black and white over my head,
querulous, wanting what?
    while I squint and speculate

ignorant, out of my country,
chosen hub of their wheel.
  They chance me high and low,
talking in bird Welsh. And having
passed all comment
innocent and outrageous, and having
satisfied themselves of my
look and my intent, both species spin out,
leaving a dark loner.

And who might you be? I ask. But the
bird has fallen silent.
Well, if the mind isn't debtors' prison, I don't
know what is. You'll pay if you
don't pay. You'll pay if you do.
(This is a story, but then, there's
not much that isn't).

"Moore! Moore!" a jackdaw cries, for sale
from a man who robbed the nest.
Hearing his surname,
Tom Moore the linen draper buys him.
Soon the daw can glibly quote a full identity:
"Tom Moore, of Sackville Street."

Moore is fond of gambling: at a corner table
in his shop, journeymen play cards,
the caged jackdaw overhead. Yes,
Moore is fond of gambling though often
ends a loser. The players grumble; there's a suspect:

someone's marking cards. "Damn it,
how he nicks them," the jackdaw learns to say.

Eventually, less is Moore. (Sorry, I couldn't
resist). By then his daw's learned "Bad
    company, by God, bad company."
    Off they go, man and mimic, to the moldy
confines of a cell, Tom's gaming debts as
heavy as the doors that clang behind them.

"More! More!" That's your line, friends,
should you choose to hear the end. (As if
there were an end to memory or to sorrow).
But stay, let's have a glimpse of the pale deserted man,
ill with what was once called prison distemper.

Feverish Tom wanders,
imagined visitors ask: "Tell me, how
did you wind up here?"
"Bad," begins the bird, as Tom crawls
across the floor, "Bad company, by God."
And oh, the slanting light is lovely,
the bars bend in and out, wavery as his
hand working the catch on the cage.
    Company, by God. He lifts the daw,
is taken
Bad, oh bad and
damn it, Death nicks him.

    A flutter on the sill. A black
heartbeat in the blue . . . .
"Moore! Moore!" just drop one o,
there's the cry of life. You thought
I'd finished but I haven't.
The jackdaw saved its neck
when—caught with hungry companions—

                    ~

it said what it said what it said
to a gardener who set it free. What did it say?
You know that part; I leave you to
guess the gardener's questions. To imagine
the giddy toss,
that whole empire of air.

III

TRANSFORMATIONS

THE SNAKES

shed their skins and disappeared.
One ghost lies stretched beneath shade of
drainpipe, one curves under pinxter bush.
I put my grass shears down in fallen
blades and pick up those put away lives:
light as cellophane, perfect,
opened only at the mouth.
I think of one I mowed over by accident,
in twilight of early September. How it coiled,
in a knot of regret and headless,
untied its life in the grass.
(Ribbon of God, forgive me).

With sun shining through the panes
of each specific scale, and the calm interior of
what was, I think of greenhouses. Certainly
snakes are stems on which we place the
flowers of fear, but I am done with those gardens.
I am thinking of greenhouses
lying their lengths out, dependent like
snakes upon the sun, and the casting off
of what fills them season to season: poinsettias
giving way to lilies, roses yielding to chrysanthemums.

Wind lifts the lovely emptiness I hold in my hands,
recovers the moment of sinuous past, then
lets it drop. I lay the skins on grass;
I study them long. See the sun through
small panes various and beautiful.
Have patience: I am reminded also of churches,
of wanderers entering to
depart with the window colors in their robes.

THE DUST BATH

She comes upon a partridge place
made soft by repeated visits,
concavity where each bird
embraces its own cloud.

In this spot they succumb
to fevers of perpetual flux, opening
and closing in the language of the fan.
A daylight secret, yet their ritual
enacts the lunar phases:
non-being, appearance, increase,
full-being, decrease. Their moments
sealed in blank abandon,
this dust a different sky.

Some marks remain
in the font where wings
splashed in waters invisible, some
scroll for contemplation hangs
unseen in the air
as a feather writes in wind with
loosely turning quill: *Bronze,
black-bronze.*
Fox missed his rendezvous.

SHOWER

It patters upon your part and makes you shiver,
swift takeover, capturing every strand. Already
you're younger, with the dark hair to prove it;
your lids gleam, your mouth's bedewed
with drops that can't stay: minutely
hesitant, hurriedly lucid,
each waiting to kiss you. A brook runs
either side of your ears, sculpting throat, nape,
scattering over your breasts the
unclosing eyes of trout.   Urban water
from old pipes but dreaming of willows, pooling at the
bend in the arm, heading for the hips' meander.

Slick. Then slicker, till nearly kin to otters,
your own oil's subtle resist on nose, cheekbones, chin,
on your back that you reach around to
touch without knowing why. From their oarlocks,
both shoulder blades dip beneath
the current, and time has slipped

with the soap: corner-less block of amber.
   Forgotten too, are the loofah and little
tender-bristled brush, the shampoo of citrus, and white
cubicle's confines   while far below
your feet still offer bridges against flood.
   Under your arms, between your legs,
in every crease you possess,
the touch,
turning the mists of the mind thunder-colored.
   Your navel captures a zircon; at a place behind one knee
drops strike a vein, there leaps that
lightning of sorrow

~

flickering in, out of your life,
and your tilt your head openmouthed,
let it enter there.

   Quick—say which among all these fallen are
your tears, what place this is and whose hands
memorize your shape? When did you renounce
air, when did water's captive voice
   deepen, change unmistakably
into high falls?

OF ROWLAND, RUINED IN THE CRASH OF '29

Note nailed to the dock where they'd
find it, and then you swim, tireless.
Farther and farther, almost in exultation.

Powerless, the shore, but not Frank Thatcher's
last remark. But water was
ever a friend, and water will erase it.

Your breath still even-paced, you dwell on
niece and nephew: first editions for Robert,
gold locket for Molly. For when they'd turn

twenty-one, and you recall your own
occasion: a tilting doorway in May moonlight,
and the party hectic

inside.   Someone came out—was it
Constance? to find out where you'd gone,
and she—but never mind. Fantastic, how their faces

flare. (Forgive me, oh my favorites). You might have
married, had your own, must go on planing to
   perfection
these strokes learned years ago

in shallows, between capable parents.
"Like scissors through silk," someone who
saw you compete once said

and you had touched—this morning—your
trophies ranged upon the shelves.
Name. Date. Wild iridescence in the tarnish.

Denial

Not flowers paled to phantoms
ready to be pitched,
nor sediment in a glass
clotting the last
mouthful of wine. Not the shirt
that missed the chair
and not that
clock beheading seconds

but windows, north-facing,
twin voids of unspeakable twilight.

Fine
until you face them, those tall
masters of erasure
turn their blue dials,
        slowly occlude the room.
In thickened air a diminutive autumn:
descent of transparent petals
falling, in odd numbers,
upon the table's dark pond
while the clock's insane *so what   so what*
looms and recedes.

Now you may drink from the
glass that mocks you
        good while it lasted,
warp with tears
the reach of one contorted
white sleeve.

Cheri's Telling Stories

    her elbows resting on a tea towel
folded thrice for padding on the surface of a
table round and oak, that was her mother's,
companioned by a cabinet: bow front gorged with china,
that listens at her back.

She circles, passenger in a plane that's
dumping fuel, the pilot's doing his best but it looks like
they're not going to make it. The bay is close,
she's thinking: *if I live through this*
I'll go by train, I'll never set foot on another plane and
    before she managed Little Richard
he was picking up tables with his teeth (photo
reveals him, leonine, his smile 300 watts) and God!
that was ugly furniture, bought in his first
buying spree and Tutti Frutti? they were just
kidding around, he seized on something she said
    and when that girl tried to borrow
carbolic acid from her uncle
he gave her a narrow look, asked her what
she wanted it for. She said: "To take out a spot," but he'd
divined her trouble, sent her away gently, she later
gave birth to a boy. "Hello Spot,"
he said when he first saw the child. No one knew
why but the girl and the man who fathered
the child. Shame she must bear but at least
she didn't die for her folly. "Hello Spot,"
he said it lovingly, versed in human frailty

~

        we leave him for her gambling father
heading west in an open wagon. Fate lets fall
a card (white glimpse in endless air), points at the
restless man, turns a ring on her finger. Blizzard sets in;
they find him five days later. Frozen.
His betting's over, the hour grows late and

cigarette smoke serpentines above
her little flying hands, her face—the skin
café au lait—liberally freckled, her dark hair
loosened, the cat in her voice
    Siamese.
        No one's tired, we five
haven't a clue where she'll take us next,
know only that we've got the ticket.

DAVID
—DSM 1913 - 1992

When black was not black enough,
you left the ink uncapped,
distilling by evaporation a deeper
night from your bottle of Higgins, the
better to shock against white. With
        or against your certitude of line, washes
of chosen greys controlled and
refined by wetness laid down in
swathes. Someone (if someone watched),
might find in your timing   more than a trace of
hemorrhage and horse race. It was all
outpouring, it was unstoppable ink's advance
abruptly or by melting half tones halted
        through areas left dry or deftly dampened,
decreed by you,
lord of loose order and strict chance.

Blank no longer, paper yielded sweep of
tufted field and sky, maybe women who were
cellos paired with cats in porkpie hats.
Cornfields: their edges stitched with train
trestle. Saxophones note-swapping amid
nightclub smoke. Worlds stark and worlds sensual;
music's got to travel.

  Say what of the nib? Burnt rib,
   black with crackle.
  And of the brush? Lush, honey, lush.
  There's a confidence born of
  need to burn the past and lick the future
  with as much mercurial
  fury as present will allow.

~

Commissions only. Gigs that paid.
You dipped again into the Higgins.
Shut, for a moment, your eyes
to hear whatever paper whispered. Swiftly
they arrived: musicians,
dancers, actors, and plain people of everyday just
looking out a window
or walking somewhere, cooking,
hovering over chess games, locked within
embraces illicit or sanctified. You never judged,
merely made them people we'd recognize:
ourselves, in our own shoes,
in situations where the wise were sometimes
present, or in others where whiff
of danger promised disaster or where
caution in any form had been abandoned to
movement, laughter,
or to sorrow, double-bent.

   Hundreds. Stoked by rhythms of the jazz you
loved best: something that
swung, something resilient of time's test.

Voodoo

When he found it, we said let it alone,
call the police. But he tampered with it,
took money out before a squad car arrived.
Baffled, the officers grew annoyed,
made accusations of hoax, and he
protested, saying he found it while walking
on the beach. And I can tell you that
was true, and the officers took the bag away.

What do you believe in?
That night, the electrical blew.
In the blacked-out house were three who—
not long after—died in succession.
The two who lived there were
ill already, but the third died accidentally,
in waters of a lake in another state.

What can I tell you? Ignorance of that world
allows me only this:
the bag was blue cloth that held a
wealth of wrapped candies,
money—all in coins—and the dead
sea bird, head doubled back on its body.
Placed not on lawn but sand. Low wall and road
between. Aligned with the door of the house.

There was a room there I never
slept in well, entered with reluctance.
Place that birthed malaise, a feeling of
being watched. Where wind in the narrow
corridor between that house and the next,
sang of something thwarted. Where fog horn
oppressed when elsewhere it pleased.

~

Some speak of energy, auras. How
dwellings soak them up. I'll say
I do not think that house had been happy
for some years. We loved its people
though their own love kept each other
captive. New links every year. Too proud and
interdependent, they grew isolated there.
Illness came; there were no friends close by
who knew enough to care. Help was hired—
different women—and out of them came one
who knew of rituals none of us knew.

Pieces are missing, you know? Something owed,
some grudge. Or the wish to be free
at whatever cost, confessed or intuited.
    She was a woman who knew of a man.
Or a woman in touch through
another woman. Right there
in town. Be careful what you ask for.
What is summoned will be strong.
What comes can't be sent away.

Yet we'd had good times there, sitting
round the table. We'd loved them, tried to help,
and near the end we sensed a rage
so palpable it was the furniture, the art work
and the walls: a darkness where love unraveled
and the house tensed itself and then
that person entered their lives,
went away and returned.
            Morning arrived;
Long Island Sound looked flat and calm.
The bag lay on the beach.

CAKE

Barge of my life, you drift forward, ablaze.
Sweet thing, afloat in the hands of a friend.

No singing, only the years—she has lit them all—
Arranged in formal rows around a paper picture, and

Sugar violets, vivid, with two-dot yellow stares
That draw me back to woods of childhood; I sit

Weakly in my chair, stricken shy again.
Around me, company bids me to be wind.

I blow first strong then tremulous on this
Tiny stand of trees, topped with

Vernal promise, the increase of the light.
A year I nearly drowned stays lit,

The heavy losses end in hisses. There's wavering.
Some survivors. Brief moment in which I,

Wrapped in a boa of smoke,
Observe these waxen ranks. Here's my

Chronology, those dice rolls: live die live die
And the future strobing whitely should I dare

To close my eyes, bear down like my
mother giving birth, omniscient for a moment.

Cup

It's not funny at all to your mother,
but you laugh and laugh.
What else to make of this
arc of juice,
your sudden power?

Cup! You can't say it,
but stridently can crow.
Can't say *gavel, court*, but close
case with lusty banging.

Shriek of cockatiel. Lift. Let
fall. Thrilling contact when thing
resounds with metallic thock!
Again. Again.

Fine game until She looms, her
hand large, largest of all.
Cloth comes at you—moist, horrid—
chair and tray cinch you in,
turn you tyrant in this land

that often aches with unreason.
Mine, you'd say, could you
say it, but trust instead to a
vowel. Clutch hard the shiny.
Intent to have your way.

Spoon

Something of wave cresting, of dolphin's
brow, and scallop shell skimming
Venus toward shore: sea shapes for a handle's
end, while below your three initials
link in the manner of grapevine.

At stem's end preceding bowl, the
scallop imprint again, then comes the
bowl itself, nearly goose egg-sized. You did not
eat from this but stirred, then served among the plates
something choice for Sunday's meal.
I would name it, but dwell instead upon your
mouth, its many wisdoms. How when you laughed
you opened wide to let the sound
round out.   The seas of time have rolled us
apart, together, apart. I shall never be
done with your abundance (yours, my own,
yours) until that long-gathering wave.
(Know I have picked a green hill).

Scratches, a nick near the letter L
speak of use; one edge has worn from circling
clockwise. Right-handed, you
drew strokes inward to yourself. Your love?
Your love was outward.

What does it mean to hold it? Cool, shapely
weight whose heft and balance pleases,
yet carries incarnate that triumph of
objects over flesh. I shall raise it in gnarled hands
years from today, divining from its sterling
something I heard you say.

Plate

Bearing soufflés that made the cloud-makers
proud, however they might have fretted before
company came. Warmed repeatedly
in the oven, till the porcelain crazed.

   My dear, this plate is yours, but have a care
for what you inherit: three generations of women,
dish towels in hand. Like the mythical hare of Japan,
they seemed to be polishing the moon.
   Hypnosis of circles, smaller and smaller: they rubbed it
dry. The plate waned,
waxed, suddenly *was* the moon. They saw their faces
staring back and they
                        went under. And
   deep was the lake they discovered. Wading out they
swam when they could
   no longer stand. Oh, the lake,
finally theirs; they struck out with bold
strokes
   so when a voice brought them back
they turned, unseeing. Made no answer
but placed, bitterly, plate within rack. They

pushed open the screen door, went wistfully
out back. They stood straining to hear
again the silence of somewhere else.
To strip. Enter in.

My fable. Old, not modern, yes?
Still, think on what I've said.

WILD TURKEY EGG

Easy to say unless you're carrying one by mouth.
But the carrier quit near golden oregano
growing by the milk house. There lay the egg,
its pallor set off by the chartreuse of
the herb. And it was whitish-dun. Flecked, but barely.

You found it, and we set to generating theories.
Yours was Victorian: ball & claw, the egg swooped up
in talons. I said no, that couldn't be, something
startled a raccoon. Then you confessed to viewing Mars
in the dark of 4 a.m. What's that old phrase?
"T'was meet and fitting." Enter my theory, astride
your astrological sign. You were born
mid-April; Mars looms as close as we'll
ever see it: the closest approach between the
two planets in recorded history. Pre-dawn, you'd
    slipped out,
stood in silent homage: All hail, Sky Garnet.
Greetings, Locus of Sci-Fi.

I want, I said, to save the shell. Leave it by the
    kitchen
sink. I'll open up that broken spot, let the yolk
drain out. I had my breakfast, came back in,
chose among spoons for surgery, but the egg seemed
bigger; something dark resisted from within.
Squeamish, I asked your help,
and we took it outside. (Reader, observe my husband,
The Beak. See the break-in widen).

Wow. What fell out. Dinosaur. Changeling. Gryphon.
Imperial Local. Plain Ordinary, sheathed in
                    ~

dumb power. Released from egg-world to the other,
the chick enlarged to twice its size.
"Short flight, non-stop," quipped Death disguised
(a Blade among blades).
Around the toes of our shoes lay lovely
semi-gloss bits.
Heads inclined, we felt the
heat of the sun. We spoke but little.

THE CHANCE

Light on a glossy wall: a nymph's pool,
rippling. Pale chair a boat adrift
on the lake of wide-planked floor.

Beyond glass, operas of leaves
fan the house; they cease,
become cloisonné leaves set in blue enamel.

Such stillness. How long that cloud
keeps its pure, untroubled brow.
Before lengthening.   Before leaving.

I hear what cannot be heard: lungs of
eternity working, drawn from my own
breathfuls as I lie on our rumpled bed,

your touch still upon me,
though you've risen and left the room,
the air seismic with pleasure and memory

the cracks widening and widening, and I see us
layered, lover on lover (have we been others?).
Late sun and gilt mirror

flash the futile imperative:
last,   last
And again they enter each other.

EVENING

Sky, preserve your brightness while we shun
tally of these trees, yet somehow
register the silhouette of every topmost leaf.

Among mint's blossomed spires, the hawk moth's
petit point, while from a place we cannot locate,
some tremolant note, over and over.

Bumblebee dying slowly in the lap of a lily.
(Jewel of industry   Yes,   rest). Crusades:
young grapes caught up in tendrils' quest.

Dropped trowel, wayward rake, gleam of
galvanized can. And moonlight soon, greenish
on the grey of the mounting block. Tell me

don't tell me you love me as we turn towards
the house. One window lit, the rest outfacing us
with blank, resistant stares. Here come those

tiny tiles, the blurred set among the clear.
One and one and one Night sings, thrilled with
restoration. One hundred hues of blue to be lost in

so give me your hand.

SELKIE

A single line would occupy him for many days.
—Vernon Watkins
Letters Of Dylan Thomas to Vernon Watkins

Ah yes, the single line.
From where I attempt to write this
she suns herself at a distance,
sleek upon rock, beautifully blent
with that warm shade. The stretch of
sea between us. Oh, keel furrowing sand, you
make too obvious
    my intent. But I have embarked.

My dory leaks. I carry with me my usual
flask of tears. (Rarely a swig, friends,
rarely a swig). I've a fish sandwich and always,
my inability to swim. Something ails the left
    oarlock, makes my rowing sore, and the sun—
beset by mist—in sullen alchemy makes lead
from waves that earlier shone

pewter. My prow hammers; I'm
aware the line has changed, lovely as I am
awkward; I'll never catch her this way.
My net has holes, it was ever thus,
yet must I row for a glimpse. One look of
recognition, cruel as any club.

    She left—in slipping off—the darkest spot
upon the rock. I fend off. The mist thickens.

~

    Yet I have known her now, and I
know nothing. Fathoms and fathoms she swims
as I row back. Swash of the shallows, cold about
my ankles. I've a grain of sand between
two molars, and I grind it there. One bubble escaped
from her mouth has somehow entered my ear.
A month may pass; a night will
come, whitely illumined,
and in another form she will be
given me on shore.

The Name On The Cup

You refused it early on—
four syllables, stress on the second—
for something humbler,
shorter by two,
stress on the first. But that
was later, this cup recalls
the era of language skidding
by, slick-handled, out of
reach. Therefore you drummed. Trilled
music of brinksmanship,
and your grasp strengthened with your
voice, that would one day
mesmerize.

Here your first creations survive:
seven dents, bottom-side. Two crescents in homage
(after pointing awestruck at the moon). One
hoofprint of defiance (trifle not with me!).
Four seals set (behold this toothless mirth,
my thirst, my hunger. And deepest, this:
my cloudless gaze).
Beneath the circlet of letters engraved
with the lilt and swoop of
goldfinch flight, they catch the tarnish, darken.

Bright well of milk, of water. Always
your way was your own. You drank
up, you laughed and spilled, becoming someone else.
The name you rejected in time found
renaissance, cut in rose granite
while the other leaps, as yet indelible,
living upon my tongue.

Notes

"Work" and "For Sale": The water wheel and church mentioned in these poems are in Merthyr Mawr, included with the Porthcawl group by virtue of close proximity.

"Note for a Field Without House": Porthcawl, South Wales, is tropic enough in climate to support palm trees.

"Tribute": The poem is loosely based on an event honoring poet Roland Mathias during the Hay-on-Wye Festival of 2003.

"Jackdaw": The poem draws on the Celtic story of the same name. The variant I know, I found in *Irish Fairy & Folk Tales,* edited by W. B. Yeats. "Daw" is a colloquial substitute for jackdaw. I've added an *e* to the end of Tom Moor's name to serve a specific line in the poem.

"David": Illustrator David Stone Martin changed the record album industry with his innovative covers. Drawings of jazz musicians represent his best known oeuvre and graced the covers of Norgran, Clef, Verve, and others.

"Of Rowland, Ruined in the Crash of '29: Rowland was a great uncle on my mother's side, reputed to be a superb swimmer. My mother and my uncle Robert were Rowland's cherished niece and nephew, and he their favorite uncle. My uncle provided me with his own version of Rowland's suicide. In preserving what is partial mystery I've embellished slightly.

"Selkie": In Celtic folk tale, selkies traditionally straddle two worlds. By day they are seals out in the sea, but at night swim in to shed sealskins on the beach and frolic in human form. If a woman loses possession of her sealskin to a mortal man, she is bound to him, tied to life on land unless she can get her sealskin back.

About the Author

Margot Farrington is the author of two collections of poetry,
and her poems have been included in several anthologies.
Other writings include essays, and reviews of poetry books
and art exhibitions. Steeped in theater—her earliest love—she
has widely read and performed her work, both as poet and as
storyteller. She has presented many literary events, both in
the New York City area and Upstate.

About the Book

The type and layout of *Flares and Fathoms* were designed by
Bertha Rogers, as was the cover. The artwork on the cover is a
painting by Tony Martin, "Departure of Whim." The typeface
for the text and cover is Adobe InDesign CS Arrus Book Type.
The book was printed on 60-lb. offset, acid-free, recycled
paper in the United States of America. This first edition is
limited to copies in paper wrappers.

OTHER BRIGHT HILL PRESS BOOKS

POETRY AND FICTION COLLECTIONS

The Aerialist, **Victoria Hallerman $12**
2003 Poetry Book Award - Chosen by Martin Mitchell
Bright Hill Press Poetry Book Award Series

LightsOut, **Tom Lavazzi $6**
Second Place, 2003 Poetry Chapbook Award
Bright Hill Press At Hand Poetry Chapbook Series

Walking Back the Cat, **Lynn Pattison** *(forthcoming)* **$6**
Third Place, 2003 Poetry Chapbook Award
Bright Hill Press At Hand Poetry Chapbook Series

The Spirit of the Walrus, **ElisaVietta Ritchie** *(forthcoming)* **$6**
Fourth Place, 2003 Poetry Chapbook Award
Bright Hill Press At Hand Poetry Chapbook Series

Web-Watching, Bruce Bennett **$6**
2003 Poetry Chapbook Award
Bright Hill Press At Hand Poetry Chapbook Series

Strange Gravity, **Lisa Rhoades $12**
2002 Poetry Book Award - Chosen by Elaine Terranova
Bright Hill Press Poetry Book Award Series

Possum, **Shelby Stephenson $6**
2002 Poetry Chapbook Award
Bright Hill Press At Hand Poetry Chapbook Series

First Probe to Antarctica, **Barry Ballard $6**
2001 Poetry Chapbook Award
Bright Hill Press At Hand Poetry Chapbook Series

The Singer's Temple, **Barbara Hurd $12**
2001 Poetry Book Award - Chosen by Richard Frost
Bright Hill Press Poetry Book Award Series

Inspiration Point, **Matthew J. Spireng $6**
2000 Poetry Chapbook Award
Bright Hill Press At Hand Poetry Chapbook Series

OTHER BRIGHT HILL PRESS TITLES *(cont.)*

ANTHOLOGIES & OTHERS

Fantastic! The Word Thursdays
Workshops for Kids 2004-05 Anthology (forthcoming) $12
Edited by Bertha Rogers - BH Books by and for Kids

Bright Hill Book Arts 2004 $12
Edited by Bertha Rogers
Bright Hill Exhibition Series

Bright Hill Book Arts 2003 $10
Edited by Bertha Rogers
Bright Hill Exhibition Series

On the Watershed: The Natural World
of New York's Catskill Mountain Region $14.95
Poetry & Prose by Catskill Student Writers, Illustrated
Edited by Bertha Rogers

The Second Word Thursdays Anthology $19.95
Poetry, Fiction, & Nonfiction by Word Thursdays Authors
Edited by Bertha Rogers

The WT Summer & Winter Workshops for Kids
1998 Anthology $10
BH Books by and for Kids - Edited by Bertha Rogers

Iroquois Voices, Iroquois Visions $12
Edited by Bertha Rogers - Contributing Editors
Robert Bensen, Maurice Kenny, Tom Huff

Out of the Catskills & Just Beyond $24.95
Literary & Visual Works by Catskill Writers & Artists,
with a Special Section by Catskill High-School Writers & Artists
Edited by Bertha Rogers

The Word Thursdays Anthology
Edited by Bertha Rogers

Speaking the Words Anthology
Edited by Bertha Rogers

ORDERING BRIGHT HILL PRESS BOOKS *(see order form below)*

BOOKSTORES: Bright Hill Press books are distributed to the trade by Small Press Distribution, 1814 San Pablo Ave., Berkeley, CA 94702-1624; Baker & Taylor, 44 Kirby Ave., POB 734, Somerville, NJ 08876-0734; and North Country Books (regional titles), 311 Turner St., POB 217, Utica, NY 13501-1727. Our books may also be found at BarnesandNoble.com and Amazon.com.

INDIVIDUALS: If your local bookstores do not stock Bright Hill Press books, please ask them to special order, or write to us at Bright Hill Press, POB 193, Treadwell, NY 13846-0193 or to our e-mail address: wordthur@stny.rr.com, or by telephone at 607-829-5055. Further information may be found on our web site: www.brighthillpress.org.

ORDER FORM *(This page may be duplicated)*

Title____ Quantity______Price____

Title ____ Quantity______Price____

Title ____ Quantity______Price____

Title ____ Quantity______Price____

Shipping & Handling_______________SubTotal__________

Sales Tax____________________________

New York State Residents, and where Applicable. Note: We cannot process orders without payment of applicable sales tax. (Orders of 3 or more, subtract 20% from total before sales tax.)

Member discount (Subtract 10% from total before sales tax)________

Ship to_______________________________________

Address____

City_____________________________________State_________Zip Code________

CHECK OR MONEY ORDER: AMT ENCL. $______________

(total includes price of book(s), plus shipping & applicable taxes)

MasterCard____________ VISA____________

Card Account Number____

Card Expiration Date____________________________________

Customer Signature____

Customer Tele. #___________________________E-mail__________________________

Card-issuing Bank Name____